MAD LIBS JUNIOR™

By Roger Price and Leonard Stern

PSS!

PRICE STERN SLOAN

PRICE STERN SLOAN
Published by the Penguin Group
Penguin Group (USA) Inc., 375 Hudson Street, New York, New York 10014, U.S.A.
Penguin Group (Canada), 90 Eglinton Avenue East, Suite 700, Toronto, Ontario, Canada M4P 2Y3
(a division of Pearson Penguin Canada Inc.)
Penguin Books Ltd, 80 Strand, London WC2R 0RL, England
Penguin Ireland, 25 St Stephen's Green, Dublin 2, Ireland
(a division of Penguin Books Ltd)
Penguin Group (Australia), 250 Camberwell Road, Camberwell, Victoria 3124, Australia
(a division of Pearson Australia Group Pty Ltd)
Penguin Books India Pvt Ltd, 11 Community Centre, Panchsheel Park, New Delhi – 110 017, India
Penguin Group (NZ), Cnr Airborne and Rosedale Roads, Albany, Auckland 1310, New Zealand
(a division of Pearson New Zealand Ltd)
Penguin Books (South Africa) (Pty) Ltd, 24 Sturdee Avenue, Rosebank, Johannesburg 2196, South Africa

Penguin Books Ltd, Registered Offices:
80 Strand, London WC2R 0RL, England

Mad Libs format copyright © 2007 by Price Stern Sloan.

ISBN 978-0-8431-2136-0

3 5 7 9 10 8 6 4 2

MAD LIBS JUNIOR.
INSTRUCTIONS

MAD LIBS JUNIOR™ is a game for kids who don't like games!
It can be played by one, two, three, four, or forty.

RIDICULOUSLY SIMPLE DIRECTIONS:

At the top of each page in this book, you will find four columns of words, each headed by a symbol. Each symbol represents a part of speech. The symbols are:

★	☺	➔	?
NOUNS	ADJECTIVES	VERBS	MISC.

MAD LIBS JUNIOR™ is fun to play with friends, but you can also play it by yourself! To begin, look at the story on the page below. When you come to a blank space in the story, look at the symbol that appears underneath. Then find the same symbol on this page and pick a word that appears below the symbol. Put that word in the blank space, and cross out the word, so you don't use it again. Continue doing this throughout the story until you've filled in all the spaces. Finally, read your story aloud and laugh!

EXAMPLE:

"Good-bye!" he said, as he jumped into his _____ and _____
                                                         ★   ➔

off with his pet _____ .
                           ?

★	☺	➔	?
NOUNS	ADJECTIVES	VERBS	MISC.
car	curly	drove	hamster
boat	purple	~~danced~~	dog
roller skate	wet	drank	cat
taxicab	tired	twirled	~~giraffe~~
~~airplane~~	silly	swam	monkey

"Good-bye!" he said, as he jumped into his ___AIRPLANE___ and ___DANCED___
                                                              ★   ➔

off with his pet ___GIRAFFE___ .
                           ?

In case you haven't learned about the parts of speech yet, here is a quick lesson:

A **NOUN** ★ is the name of a person, place, or thing. *Sidewalk, umbrella, bathtub,* and *roller blades* are nouns.

An **ADJECTIVE** ☺ describes a person, place, or thing. *Lumpy, soft, ugly, messy,* and *short* are adjectives.

A **VERB** ➜ is an action word. *Run, jump,* and *swim* are verbs.

MISC. ? can be any word at all. Some examples of a word that could be miscellaneous are: *nose, monkey, five,* and *blue.*

Say It Two Ways!

¡Actívate!	Activate!
¡Al rescate!	To the rescue!
¡Amigo! (for a boy)	Friend!
¡Amiga! (for a girl)	Friend!
¡Ayúdame!	Help me!
¡Ayúdanos!	Help us!
¡De nada!	You're welcome!
¡Gracias!	Thank you!
¡Hasta luego!	So long!
¡Hola!	Hello!
¡Mami!	Mother!
¡Mira!	Look!
¡Misión cumplida!	Rescue complete!
¡Muchas gracias!	Thanks very much!
¡Muy bien!	Great!
¡Nada!	Swim!
¡Salta!	Jump!
¡Sube!	Climb!

MAD LIBS JUNIOR™ is fun to play with friends, but you can also play it by yourself! To begin, look at the story on the page below. When you come to a blank space in the story, look at the symbol that appears underneath. Then find the same symbol on this page and pick a word that appears below the symbol. Put that word in the blank space, and cross out the word, so you don't use it again. Continue doing this throughout the story until you've filled in all the spaces. Finally, read your story aloud and laugh!

THE MYSTERIOUS EGG, PART 1

★ NOUNS	☺ ADJECTIVES	➡ VERBS	? MISC.
pirate	pretty	skipping	arooooo
hamster	puffy	sliding	sizzzzle
flea	hungry	leaping	whomp
unicorn	lonely	driving	crrreaack
dragon	rubbery	flying	uhuhu
clown	shiny	swinging	gigglegoo
refrigerator	sunny	hang-gliding	moooo
alien	drippy	spinning	eeorrrr
brontosaurus	lumpy	grunting	hatchaaa
garbage truck	goofy	bopping	whackadoo
robot	sloppy	hula-hooping	zzzzz
wizard	adorable	hopping	ssssss

Diego and Baby Jaguar were _____ through the

_____ mountains when they saw a/an _____

egg _____ at their feet. "How did that egg get here?" asked

Baby Jaguar. "What kind of egg is it?" Diego asked. "I wonder if it's a/an

_____ egg," said Baby Jaguar. "We should check the Field

Journal," said Diego. "It could belong to a/an _____."

"The egg is making a/an _____ noise!" said Baby Jaguar.

"_____," went the egg. Then it started _____

with a soft "_____." "It's hatching!" said Diego. Suddenly,

with a loud "_____," the egg cracked open. "That's no

_____," said Diego. "It's an Andean flamingo!" "*Hola*, Baby

Flamingo," Baby Jaguar said. "Don't worry—we'll help you find your *mami*."

MAD LIBS JUNIOR™ is fun to play with friends, but you can also play it by yourself! To begin, look at the story on the page below. When you come to a blank space in the story, look at the symbol that appears underneath. Then find the same symbol on this page and pick a word that appears below the symbol. Put that word in the blank space, and cross out the word, so you don't use it again. Continue doing this throughout the story until you've filled in all the spaces. Finally, read your story aloud and laugh!

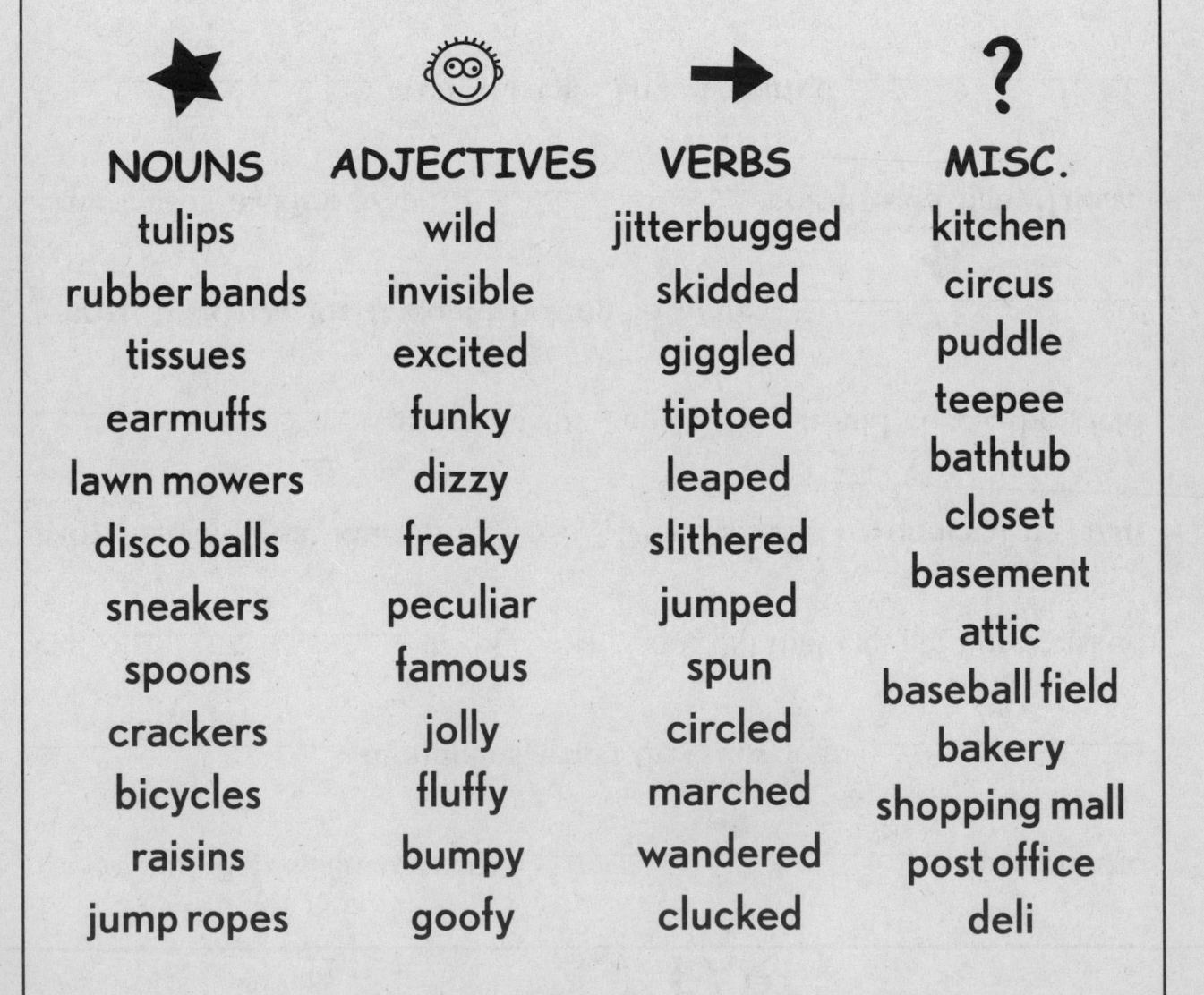

THE MYSTERIOUS EGG, PART 2

★ NOUNS	☺ ADJECTIVES	➜ VERBS	? MISC.
tulips	wild	jitterbugged	kitchen
rubber bands	invisible	skidded	circus
tissues	excited	giggled	puddle
earmuffs	funky	tiptoed	teepee
lawn mowers	dizzy	leaped	bathtub
disco balls	freaky	slithered	closet
sneakers	peculiar	jumped	basement
spoons	famous	spun	attic
crackers	jolly	circled	baseball field
bicycles	fluffy	marched	bakery
raisins	bumpy	wandered	shopping mall
jump ropes	goofy	clucked	post office
			deli

MAD LIBS JUNIOR
THE MYSTERIOUS EGG, PART 2

Diego used his Video Watch to contact Alicia at the Animal Rescue Center. "I

know Andean flamingos don't live in the _____**?**," said Diego,

"but where do they live?" Alicia's _____☺ computer had the answer.

"Go past the _____★ in the _____**?** to the lake on top

of the mountain," she told Diego. *"Gracias,"* he said. *"¡Al rescate!* To the

rescue!" he called to Baby Jaguar and the flamingo. Diego led the way.

They _____➡ past _____★ and _____➡ around

_____★. Finally, they climbed the mountain and found the flamingos.

"¡Mami!" called Baby Flamingo. "My baby!" exclaimed a/an _____☺

flamingo. "When your egg _____➡ away, I thought I'd never see you

again! *Muchas gracias*, Diego." Seeing Baby Flamingo and his *mami*

together made Diego as happy as a bug in a/an _____**?**.

MAD LIBS JUNIOR™ is fun to play with friends, but you can also play it by yourself! To begin, look at the story on the page below. When you come to a blank space in the story, look at the symbol that appears underneath. Then find the same symbol on this page and pick a word that appears below the symbol. Put that word in the blank space, and cross out the word, so you don't use it again. Continue doing this throughout the story until you've filled in all the spaces. Finally, read your story aloud and laugh!

WORKING WITH CLICK

★ NOUNS	☺ ADJECTIVES	→ VERBS	? MISC.
fingernail	happy	squeaking	nose
piano	fuzzy	skating	ear
movie star	cute	shimmying	belly button
ladder	lumpy	giggling	foot
muffin	polka-dotted	cartwheeling	elbow
sneaker	silly	wiggling	knee
papaya	jittery	dancing	thumb
birthday cake	slimy	hopping	head
potato	itty-bitty	crawling	forehead
lily pad	shaggy	spinning	brain
telephone	wacky	twirling	eyeball
fire truck	tricky	somersaulting	rib cage

Diego heard a sound that went like this: *"Eeeeeiiiieee!"* "Oh, no!" he cried.

"That sounds like an animal in trouble!" Diego went _____ ➡️

up to the Science Deck so Click the Camera could help him find the animal.

"*Hola*, Click. Where is the _____ 😊 animal in trouble?" "Let's

zoom through the forest," said Click, showing Diego a/an _____ 😊

picture. But all Diego could see was a _____ ⭐. Click zoomed in.

"Look, Diego," Click said. "That is the animal's _____❓"

"Right," said Diego. "That animal can camouflage itself so it can go

_____ ➡️ through the treetops." *"Eeeeeiiiiee!"* the animal

called again, _____ ➡️ on its _____❓. "Oh!" said

Diego. "I thought its _____❓ was a _____⭐! I hope

it keeps _____ ➡️ so I can find it when I reach the rain forest!"

MAD LIBS JUNIOR™ is fun to play with friends, but you can also play it by yourself! To begin, look at the story on the page below. When you come to a blank space in the story, look at the symbol that appears underneath. Then find the same symbol on this page and pick a word that appears below the symbol. Put that word in the blank space, and cross out the word, so you don't use it again. Continue doing this throughout the story until you've filled in all the spaces. Finally, read your story aloud and laugh!

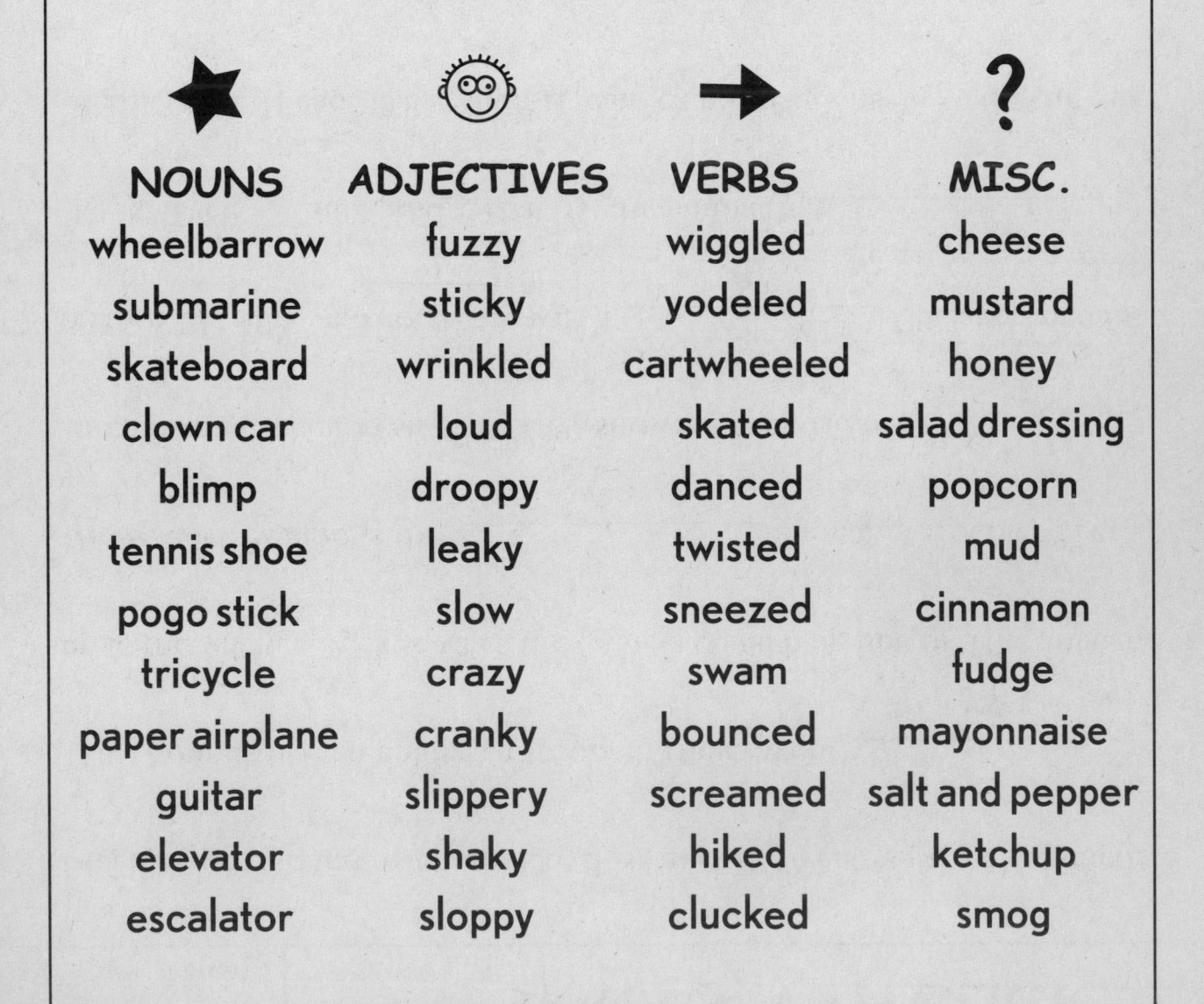

WILD WEATHER, PART 1

★ NOUNS	☺ ADJECTIVES	➡ VERBS	? MISC.
wheelbarrow	fuzzy	wiggled	cheese
submarine	sticky	yodeled	mustard
skateboard	wrinkled	cartwheeled	honey
clown car	loud	skated	salad dressing
blimp	droopy	danced	popcorn
tennis shoe	leaky	twisted	mud
pogo stick	slow	sneezed	cinnamon
tricycle	crazy	swam	fudge
paper airplane	cranky	bounced	mayonnaise
guitar	slippery	screamed	salt and pepper
elevator	shaky	hiked	ketchup
escalator	sloppy	clucked	smog

MAD LIBS JUNIOR
WILD WEATHER, PART 1

"*¡Ayúdame!*" Alicia called to Diego on the Video Watch. "I _____ ➡

through the _____ **?** in the rain forest to rescue a pygmy

marmoset. But after I found it, we got caught in a _____ **?**

storm!" Diego _____ ➡ on his _____ ⭐, heading into

the rain forest to help. He _____ ➡ into the _____ **?**

until he was stopped by a giant puddle filled with _____ 😊 mud.

"I'll need Rescue Pack to get across," Diego said. What should Rescue Pack

transform into? Would a/an _____ ⭐ help Diego? Or a

_____ 😊 _____ ⭐? "*¡Actívate!*" he shouted, and

Rescue Pack became a _____ 😊 plane. "Good thinking, Rescue

Pack," Diego said as he easily _____ ➡ over the mud. He was

one step closer to finding Alicia and the pygmy marmoset.

MAD LIBS JUNIOR™ is fun to play with friends, but you can also play it by yourself! To begin, look at the story on the page below. When you come to a blank space in the story, look at the symbol that appears underneath. Then find the same symbol on this page and pick a word that appears below the symbol. Put that word in the blank space, and cross out the word, so you don't use it again. Continue doing this throughout the story until you've filled in all the spaces. Finally, read your story aloud and laugh!

WILD WEATHER, PART 2

★ NOUNS	☺ ADJECTIVES	→ VERBS	? MISC.
noodle	angry	flying	butter
toothpick	plump	surfing	hot sauce
tomato	stinky	screaming	lemonade
fire truck	neon	screeching	milk
artichoke	cranky	yodeling	chili
washing machine	spotted	swimming	sawdust
doughnut	yummy	waltzing	orange juice
yoyo	slinky	humming	apple sauce
spoon	rubbery	sneezing	fruit punch
picnic basket	mushy	leapfrogging	glue
wig	pickled	buzzing	gravy
bow tie	spiky	fluttering	lettuce

Diego found Alicia and the pygmy marmoset stuck in a/an _____

tree. All the _____ **?** on the ground made it impossible for them

to go _____ ➡ down. "How did you get up there?" Diego yelled.

"The pygmy marmoset got caught on this _____ branch," Alicia

called. "I climbed a rope to bring him down, but when the _____ **?**

started pouring, I lost my grip." Diego wrapped his sturdy _____ ★

around the tree and began climbing. He wiped the _____ **?** out

of his eyes to see where he was going. "*¡Sube!*" Alicia called. Up Diego

climbed. At last, he reached Alicia and the pygmy marmoset and helped

them to the ground. And finally, the _____ **?** stopped falling.

"*Gracias*, Diego," said Alicia and the pygmy marmoset, giving Diego a huge,

_____ hug.

MAD LIBS JUNIOR™ is fun to play with friends, but you can also play it by yourself! To begin, look at the story on the page below. When you come to a blank space in the story, look at the symbol that appears underneath. Then find the same symbol on this page and pick a word that appears below the symbol. Put that word in the blank space, and cross out the word, so you don't use it again. Continue doing this throughout the story until you've filled in all the spaces. Finally, read your story aloud and laugh!

THE MISSING WATERFALL, PART 1

★ NOUNS	☺ ADJECTIVES	→ VERBS	? MISC.
carrots	lovely	squirm	ladder
pogo sticks	grouchy	snort	playpen
sandwiches	chilly	cha-cha	puddle
nachos	crunchy	backflip	anthill
lollipops	glittery	swing	potato
backpacks	happy	bounce	four-leaf clover
bunk beds	goofy	hopscotch	mailbox
computers	friendly	tickle	roller coaster
soccer balls	rectangular	gargle	rocking chair
soda cans	outrageous	twist	toaster oven
pancakes	bumpy	flip	sand castle
peanuts	funky	sing	circus tent

Diego was about to _____ → through the _____ 😊

mountain forest back to the Animal Rescue _____ ? when he

noticed something very strange about the river. It looked like a dried-up

_____ ? ! *Where is the* _____ 😊 *water?* Diego thought.

Suddenly, he heard the familiar voice of his friend Linda the Llama. "*¡Hola,*

Diego!" she said. She was worried about the river, too. Diego used his

Spotting Scope to see through the hanging _____ ★ in

the trees to where the waterfall should be. But all he could see were

_____ ★ stacked on _____ ★ stacked on _____ ★ .

The waterfall was missing! "*¡Al rescate, amiga!*" Diego said to Linda. They

would have to hurry up and _____ → down the _____ ?

to see what happened to the waterfall.

MAD LIBS JUNIOR™ is fun to play with friends, but you can also play it by yourself! To begin, look at the story on the page below. When you come to a blank space in the story, look at the symbol that appears underneath. Then find the same symbol on this page and pick a word that appears below the symbol. Put that word in the blank space, and cross out the word, so you don't use it again. Continue doing this throughout the story until you've filled in all the spaces. Finally, read your story aloud and laugh!

THE MISSING WATERFALL, PART 2

★ NOUNS	😊 ADJECTIVES	→ VERBS	? MISC.
spaghetti	ridiculous	singing	ears
roller skates	loud	flipping	knees
lightbulbs	purple	dancing	tails
anthills	leathery	clapping	snouts
hamburgers	slick	spitting	eyebrows
coconuts	silky	hopping	teeth
forks	fuzzy	drumming	fingers
pennies	strange	parachuting	claws
pom-poms	squishy	cartwheeling	nostrils
marbles	juicy	discoing	arms
baseball cards	bumpy	sledding	backs
tubas	ticklish	wiggling	stomachs

"*¡Mira!*" said Diego when he and Linda reached the spot where the

_____ waterfall usually began. Someone had piled up

_____ to keep water from _____ into the

river. Then Diego saw the Bobo Brothers' _____

_____ _____ in the _____.

The Bobos were two _____ spider monkeys who always

caused trouble. "Freeze, Bobos!" he yelled. The Bobo Brothers stopped

_____ and said, "Sorry!" Then they went _____

off. Diego and Linda used their _____ to carry the heavy

_____. Like all llamas, Linda was strong, so she carried the

most _____. Finally, the waterfall was _____

into the river as usual. Mission accomplished!

MAD LIBS JUNIOR™ is fun to play with friends, but you can also play it by yourself! To begin, look at the story on the page below. When you come to a blank space in the story, look at the symbol that appears underneath. Then find the same symbol on this page and pick a word that appears below the symbol. Put that word in the blank space, and cross out the word, so you don't use it again. Continue doing this throughout the story until you've filled in all the spaces. Finally, read your story aloud and laugh!

THE LOST PENGUIN

★ NOUNS	☺ ADJECTIVES	➡ VERBS	? MISC.
teacups	spectacular	danced	blue-and-orange
sandwiches	itty-bitty	thumped	plaid
seashells	fizzy	spun	purple
prunes	gigantic	twirled	neon yellow
alarm clocks	slimy	gargled	pin-striped
uncles	wrinkly	flipped	polka-dotted
babysitters	lazy	screeched	hot pink
dragons	lumpy	rolled	checkered
potatoes	robotic	skipped	black-and-blue
pancakes	hairy	flapped	black-and-white
kittens	spicy	hopscotched	lime green
flowers	soupy	coughed	spotted

MAD LIBS JUNIOR
THE LOST PENGUIN

Diego was on an adventure in Antarctica. He was using his Spotting

Scope when he spied a/an _____ animal in trouble in the most

_____ part of the ocean. It was a/an _____ baby

emperor penguin, floating alone on a chunk of _____ ice.

There were no _____ around to help him! Diego _____

to the iceberg in his _____ speedboat. When he arrived, the penguin

said in a/an _____ voice, "Diego, I miss my _____ at

home." Suddenly, a/an _____ wave _____ toward

the ice. "Look out!" said Diego. Diego and the penguin _____

into the boat and _____ all the way to the baby emperor

penguin's _____ family on the _____ shores

of Antarctica. *Misión cumplida,* said Diego. "Rescue complete."

MAD LIBS JUNIOR™ is fun to play with friends, but you can also play it by yourself! To begin, look at the story on the page below. When you come to a blank space in the story, look at the symbol that appears underneath. Then find the same symbol on this page and pick a word that appears below the symbol. Put that word in the blank space, and cross out the word, so you don't use it again. Continue doing this throughout the story until you've filled in all the spaces. Finally, read your story aloud and laugh!

PEEKABOO KINKAJOU, PART 1

★ NOUNS	😀 ADJECTIVES	➡ VERBS	? MISC.
cactus	cuddly	wiggled	iiiiiiiiiiiiiee
helicopter	fuzzy	smacked	oooooooh
pineapple	squeaky	grabbed	eooorrrr
mushroom	delicious	hugged	hmmmm
balloon	smelly	hopped	sssssshhhh
snowman	rubbery	jumped	ugga-ugga
dinosaur	buttery	twirled	waaaawaa
alien	lumpy	rolled	geegeegeegee
meatball	gorgeous	tap-danced	aiiyeeee
finger puppet	fluffy	jitterbugged	mmrrrmm
bowling ball	wet	flew	clickity-click
pet rock	soggy	shook	bibblebabble

One night, Diego and Alicia were up on the Animal Rescue Center's Science

Deck when they heard a/an _____ sound outside. "What's that?"
?

Diego asked. They went to the _____ window, but it was too
☺

_____ to see. "It must be a/an _____," said Alicia, going
☺ ★

back to work on her _____. "They always go '_____' at
★ **?**

night." Then they heard a/an _____ on the window and then
?

a/an _____. "What if that's a/an _____ calling
? ★

for help?" Diego asked. He got out his _____ flashlight and
☺

_____ it at the window. He saw two _____ eyes!
➡ ☺

An animal was in the _____ outside. Alicia _____
★ ➡

closer. "Oh!" she said. "That's no _____. It's a *mami* kinkajou.
★

And I think she needs our help."

MAD LIBS JUNIOR™ is fun to play with friends, but you can also play it by yourself! To begin, look at the story on the page below. When you come to a blank space in the story, look at the symbol that appears underneath. Then find the same symbol on this page and pick a word that appears below the symbol. Put that word in the blank space, and cross out the word, so you don't use it again. Continue doing this throughout the story until you've filled in all the spaces. Finally, read your story aloud and laugh!

PEEKABOO KINKAJOU, PART 2

★ NOUNS	🙂 ADJECTIVES	➡ VERBS	? MISC.
sailboat	silly	hopped	tacos
piñata	starry	sneezed	prunes
windmill	chilly	slid	raisins
umbrella	gooey	hula-hooped	carrot sticks
radio	cheesy	twirled	lima beans
volcano	shiny	spun	brussels sprouts
Ferris wheel	wormy	itched	ice cubes
telephone	prickly	tumbled	waffles
unicycle	giggly	backstroked	sloppy joes
dictionary	sleepy	danced	onions
pickup truck	careful	jigged	artichokes
stop sign	sparkly	slipped	enchiladas

Diego and Alicia opened the window. "Mami Kinkajou," Diego said, "is

something the matter?" Mami Kinkajou _____ ➡ over to Diego.

"My _____ 😊 baby is stuck up in the _____ ⭐." Diego

used his Spotting Scope to find the _____ 😊 baby. Then he

_____ ➡ out the window and up the _____ ⭐ to rescue

him. Mami Kinkajou was happy and _____ 😊, but the baby

started to cry. "He's hungry," explained Mami Kinkajou. "Would he like

some _____ ❓?" asked Alicia. "No, *gracias*," said Mami Kinkajou.

"He loves honey, and I have some here." The baby kinkajou ate the honey

as if it were a bowl of _____ ❓ with _____ ❓ on top.

"All this rescuing made me hungry, too," said Diego. "Alicia, are there any

_____ 😊 _____ ❓ for dessert?"

MAD LIBS JUNIOR™ is fun to play with friends, but you can also play it by yourself! To begin, look at the story on the page below. When you come to a blank space in the story, look at the symbol that appears underneath. Then find the same symbol on this page and pick a word that appears below the symbol. Put that word in the blank space, and cross out the word, so you don't use it again. Continue doing this throughout the story until you've filled in all the spaces. Finally, read your story aloud and laugh!

COMPUTER GLITCH, PART 1

★ NOUNS	😊 ADJECTIVES	➡ VERBS	❓ MISC.
fork	sweaty	scuba diving	swirly green
pencil	sweet	honking	pink-and-blue
paper clip	funky	waddling	neon yellow
sock	snazzy	jiggling	metallic pink
toothbrush	dusty	spinning	black-and-white
rubber band	moldy	sizzling	checkered brown
doorknob	sleek	shrinking	orange-spotted
potato	squeaky	buzzing	pin-striped
marble	expensive	mamboing	tie-dyed
seesaw	sloppy	clapping	turquoise-spotted
pumpkin	bubbly	singing	red-and-blue
lawn mower	sticky	oinking	yellow-and-black

Diego was in the _____ layer of the rain forest searching for

a scarlet macaw that had gone _____ out of a tree. Suddenly,

the Field Journal's _____ started _____ with

a/an _____ screeching sound. Diego needed some more

information on the scarlet macaw, but the Field Journal was messing up all

the facts! It said that the scarlet macaw's feathers were _____

?

and that the red patch on its belly was _____! Diego

?

also knew that the scarlet macaw wouldn't be found munching on a

wild _____—macaws eat fruits and nuts! And scarlet

macaws definitely didn't make a sound like a/an _____

_____. "My Field Journal is not working right!" Diego

exclaimed. "It needs a new _____!"

MAD LIBS JUNIOR™ is fun to play with friends, but you can also play it by yourself! To begin, look at the story on the page below. When you come to a blank space in the story, look at the symbol that appears underneath. Then find the same symbol on this page and pick a word that appears below the symbol. Put that word in the blank space, and cross out the word, so you don't use it again. Continue doing this throughout the story until you've filled in all the spaces. Finally, read your story aloud and laugh!

COMPUTER GLITCH, PART 2

★ NOUNS	☺ ADJECTIVES	➡ VERBS	? MISC.
orangutan	gloomy	twisted	hammer
zebra	smooth	smacked	toothpick
snake	jittery	drove	garbage can
monkey	yummy	spun	tire
panda	droopy	hopped	UFO
worm	smiley	wiggled	elbow
potato	purple	honked	bagel
cougar	cuddly	clomped	diaper
wasp	disgusting	climbed	baseball bat
llama	upside-down	flipped	cuckoo clock
aardvark	frizzy	jitterbugged	flashlight
baboon	pointy	smashed	glue stick

Diego was fixing his Field Journal when he heard a/an _____ 😊

sound in the tree. The scarlet macaw _____ like a/an ➡

_____ up above. "*Hola*, Señor Macaw! I thought you were **?**

in trouble," Diego said. "No," said Señor Macaw. "But it looks like *you* need

help." Diego laughed. "My Field Journal is acting like a/an _____," ⭐

he said. Then Diego had a/an _____ idea. He removed the 😊

Field Journal's _____ chip and _____ it with a/an 😊 ➡

_____ _____. "Now it should work!" Diego said. He tested 😊 **?**

it. The Field Journal didn't say that the _____ _____ ⭐ ➡

underwater. It didn't say that the _____ lived in the ⭐

_____ part of the mountains. It said that the scarlet macaw 😊

would be found in the trees of the rain forest—which was the truth!

MAD LIBS JUNIOR™ is fun to play with friends, but you can also play it by yourself! To begin, look at the story on the page below. When you come to a blank space in the story, look at the symbol that appears underneath. Then find the same symbol on this page and pick a word that appears below the symbol. Put that word in the blank space, and cross out the word, so you don't use it again. Continue doing this throughout the story until you've filled in all the spaces. Finally, read your story aloud and laugh!

SWINGING SPIDER MONKEYS

★ NOUNS	☺ ADJECTIVES	➡ VERBS	? MISC.
pizza	super-duper	flipped	teepee
telephone	dizzy	cartwheeled	mud hut
sneaker	gooey	hula-hooped	puddle
flower	polka-dotted	giggled	tree house
pebble	silly	charged	igloo
beehive	lumpy	wiggled	gas station
papaya	hairy	bounced	volcano
piñata	crazy	leapfrogged	supermarket
radio	crunchy	waddled	sandbox
walrus	slippery	tumbled	post office
pencil	muddy	squawked	library
umbrella	gigantic	yodeled	circus

MAD LIBS JUNIOR
SWINGING SPIDER MONKEYS

The Bobo Brothers were playing with a _____ _____ 😊 ⭐

by the river. "Bobos! Bobos!" they yelled as they _____ on ➡️

rope vines high over the _____. One Bobo Brother ❓

_____ on the rope vine, pretending he was a _____ ➡️ ⭐

at the _____. The other Bobo Brother _____ over ❓ ➡️

a/an _____ with a _____ whoop of delight. ⭐ 😊

Then, the rope vines _____ out of control, and the Bobos fell ➡️

into the _____ river below. "*¡Ayúdanos!*" they yelled. Diego 😊

and Baby Jaguar _____ there quickly to rescue them. Once ➡️

they were safe, the Bobo Brothers forgot about being in _____ 😊

trouble. They _____ in the water as if they were having a ➡️

party in a/an _____. "Silly Bobos!" said Baby Jaguar and Diego. ❓

MAD LIBS JUNIOR™ is fun to play with friends, but you can also play it by yourself! To begin, look at the story on the page below. When you come to a blank space in the story, look at the symbol that appears underneath. Then find the same symbol on this page and pick a word that appears below the symbol. Put that word in the blank space, and cross out the word, so you don't use it again. Continue doing this throughout the story until you've filled in all the spaces. Finally, read your story aloud and laugh!

THE FORGOTTEN ISLAND

★ NOUNS	☺ ADJECTIVES	→ VERBS	? MISC.
radishes	fancy	cartwheeling	wallawalla
diapers	drippy	singing	oomajawa
hamsters	lumpy	thumping	lollywoo
mittens	spicy	spinning	noodlegoop
noodles	yummy	leaping	veemerjee
eyeballs	mushy	twirling	wibbleburp
race cars	fluffy	eating	bombadoobee
kitchens	slimy	dancing	fuzzamump
T-shirts	teeny-tiny	dribbling	jollyachoo
lightbulbs	wacky	hiccuping	gollihoho
flip-flops	sleepy	snorting	lumpadump
pancakes	furry	galloping	snootiwoop

Tuga the Leatherback Sea Turtle was _____ in the ocean with ➡

Diego and Alicia on her back. They had spied a _____ island 😊

off the coast of _____ that wasn't on any _____ ? 😊

map. On shore, they found statues of ancient _____. "The ⭐

_____ people carved these!" Alicia said. "Are they still here?" ?

asked Diego. Before Alicia could answer, a group of _____ 😊

native _____ started _____ out of the trees. ⭐ ➡

"_____!" they called in a strange language. They pointed to ?

Tuga in the water and said, "_____." They pointed to the ?

_____ on the sand and said, "_____." Then they ⭐ ?

pointed at themselves and said, "_____ _____." ? ?

Alicia started _____ in delight. ➡

MAD LIBS JUNIOR™ is fun to play with friends, but you can also play it by yourself! To begin, look at the story on the page below. When you come to a blank space in the story, look at the symbol that appears underneath. Then find the same symbol on this page and pick a word that appears below the symbol. Put that word in the blank space, and cross out the word, so you don't use it again. Continue doing this throughout the story until you've filled in all the spaces. Finally, read your story aloud and laugh!

A CUCKOO RESCUE, PART 1

★ NOUNS	☺ ADJECTIVES	➡ VERBS	? MISC.
unicorns	tiny	tickle	spaghetti
earmuffs	spiky	hopscotch	syrup
sneakers	wrinkly	tiptoe	rice
clowns	chewy	bop	coconut
truck drivers	sleepy	samba	honey
refrigerators	sticky	cha-cha	mustard
bananas	fuzzy	fiddle	jelly
clarinets	chunky	polka	peanut butter
beach balls	muddy	yodel	cinnamon
crayons	sparkly	tango	ketchup
trolls	fluffy	disco	mayonnaise
cowboys	hot	yawn	hot sauce

Diego, his cousin Dora the Explorer, and Boots heard a _____

sound near the _____ lake. *"Cuckoo! Cuckoo!"* They didn't

?

know if it was coming from the _____ in the weeds or the

★

_____ in the water. "Is that a _____ cuckoo or

★

a group of _____?" Boots asked. "It can't be a cuckoo,"

★

Diego said. "They _____ up north when winter is over."

➡

But when Diego, Dora, and Boots waded through the _____

?

on the shore, they found two baby black-billed cuckoos resting in the

_____. *"¡Hola!"* said Dora. "The _____ winter is

?

over. Are you lost?" "Yes," said the first cuckoo. "We were following the

_____, but they started to _____ too fast." "Will

★   ➡

you help us _____ back home?" asked the second cuckoo.

➡

MAD LIBS JUNIOR™ is fun to play with friends, but you can also play it by yourself! To begin, look at the story on the page below. When you come to a blank space in the story, look at the symbol that appears underneath. Then find the same symbol on this page and pick a word that appears below the symbol. Put that word in the blank space, and cross out the word, so you don't use it again. Continue doing this throughout the story until you've filled in all the spaces. Finally, read your story aloud and laugh!

A CUCKOO RESCUE, PART 2

★	☺	→	?
NOUNS	**ADJECTIVES**	**VERBS**	**MISC.**
cactus	icy	spinning	kitchen
mailbox	creepy	slurping	shack
eggplant	slinky	screaming	supermarket
toaster	delicious	hopping	post office
taco	smelly	grinding	attic
blimp	lumpy	coughing	basement
horn	creaky	oinking	dugout
marshmallow	sparkly	crawling	library
pumpkin	skinny	galloping	racetrack
pogo stick	slippery	sliding	sandbox
toenail	fuzzy	squeaking	castle
radio	gushy	winking	hut

"We'll help you find your _____ **?** back home," Dora told the

baby black-billed cuckoos. "Let's ask Map." Map jumped out of Backpack.

"To get to the cuckoos' home, follow the _____ 😀 path past

the _____ ⭐," said Map. "When you see the _____ 😀

_____ ⭐, start _____ ➡ until the _____ ⭐

in the sky turns _____ 😀. When you see the first _____ 😀

_____ **?**, you'll know you're home. "¡*Gracias*, Map!" said Diego.

They all traveled through the _____ 😀 _____ **?** until

they reached the _____ **?**. The cuckoos thanked Diego, Dora, Boots,

and Map by _____ ➡ out one last song. "*Cuckoo! Cuckoo!*" they

sang. Then they took off, _____ ➡ into the clouds all the way to

the _____ **?** up north that they call home. "¡*Hasta luego!*" Diego said.

MAD LIBS JUNIOR™ is fun to play with friends, but you can also play it by yourself! To begin, look at the story on the page below. When you come to a blank space in the story, look at the symbol that appears underneath. Then find the same symbol on this page and pick a word that appears below the symbol. Put that word in the blank space, and cross out the word, so you don't use it again. Continue doing this throughout the story until you've filled in all the spaces. Finally, read your story aloud and laugh!

RIDING THE RAPIDS

★ NOUNS	☺ ADJECTIVES	➡ VERBS	❓ MISC.
roller skate	funky	bounced	wonkabonka
skateboard	wiggly	twirled	aiyaeeeee
seesaw	cheesy	bopped	holeemolee
snowboard	weird	tiptoed	woweeee
school bus	delicious	yodeled	guh-guh-guh
hang glider	moldy	gobbled	yippeee
life preserver	steamy	barked	yakkety-yak
sailboat	leaky	buzzed	zzooooom
submarine	sleepy	snorted	zippadeedoo
hot-air balloon	curly	leapfrogged	hohoho
taxicab	greasy	surfed	blaaab
rocket ship	chubby	dribbled	yowza

RIDING THE RAPIDS

"_____ ?!" went a _____ 😊 cry from the raging river. A river

otter _____ ➡ in the water like an out-of-control _____ ⭐.

He was heading for the waterfall. Diego and Baby Jaguar raced to help him.

Rescue Pack _____ ➡ into the air and turned into a _____ ⭐.

Diego and Baby Jaguar _____ ➡ until they reached the rapids. The

water went _____ ? with the force of a gigantic _____ ⭐.

"_____ ?!" called the otter. He was a great swimmer, but the

current was way too _____. Diego 😊 _____ ➡ on a

_____ ⭐ and _____ ➡ into the water, and the otter

grabbed him. Then Baby Jaguar helped Diego pull the river otter out of

the water just before they reached the waterfall. "_____ ?," said

the otter gratefully. *"De nada,"* said Diego and Baby Jaguar.

MAD LIBS JUNIOR™ is fun to play with friends, but you can also play it by yourself! To begin, look at the story on the page below. When you come to a blank space in the story, look at the symbol that appears underneath. Then find the same symbol on this page and pick a word that appears below the symbol. Put that word in the blank space, and cross out the word, so you don't use it again. Continue doing this throughout the story until you've filled in all the spaces. Finally, read your story aloud and laugh!

CAMPING OUT

★ NOUNS	☺ ADJECTIVES	➡ VERBS	? MISC.
fairy	cute	cackling	iiieeeeeiie
leprechaun	prickly	snorting	wakawaka
woolly mammoth	crazy	oinking	mumblemumble
brontosaurus	lumpy	giggling	hmmmmm
pterodactyl	polka-dotted	slurping	knockknock
alien	fuzzy	croaking	hoooteewoot
elf	teeny-tiny	munching	cawcawcaw
baby dragon	glittery	screeching	snufflewuffle
unicorn	plastic	foaming	hihihihihihihi
mermaid	neon orange	neighing	sillysillysillysilly
princess	floppy	clapping	wompwomp
clown	spectacular	howling	awooooooo

One night, Diego and Alicia were camping out in the _____ 😊

forest. "_____," called an animal in the _____ 😊
?

darkness. "I wonder if that's a/an _____ _____,"
➡️   ★

Alicia said. "They're very rare." Then a/an _____ sound came
?

from up above. "Maybe that's a/an _____ _____,"
➡️   ★

Diego said. "They're so _____ that they don't even come out in
😊

the daytime." "_____," called another animal. "These are all
?

nocturnal animals," Diego said. "That means they sleep in the day and wake up

every _____ night." Alicia yawned. "All this _____
😊   ➡️

is making me sleepy," she said. "Me too," said Diego. So Diego and Alicia crawled

into their _____ tent and fell asleep to the _____
😊   ?

and _____ of their nocturnal animal friends.
?

MAD LIBS JUNIOR™ is fun to play with friends, but you can also play it by yourself! To begin, look at the story on the page below. When you come to a blank space in the story, look at the symbol that appears underneath. Then find the same symbol on this page and pick a word that appears below the symbol. Put that word in the blank space, and cross out the word, so you don't use it again. Continue doing this throughout the story until you've filled in all the spaces. Finally, read your story aloud and laugh!

CANOPY CAPERS

★ NOUNS	😊 ADJECTIVES	➡ VERBS	? MISC.
bubble	wacky	whistling	raisins
race car	wrinkly	bopping	blueberries
beanbag	sticky	cartwheeling	spaghetti
muffin	grouchy	flipping	enchiladas
tin can	wiggly	shrieking	hot peppers
piñata	slippery	dancing	lima beans
blanket	oily	hang-gliding	cheese
meatball	fluffy	skipping	popcorn
teddy bear	icky	snowboarding	lasagna
spaceship	rusty	cycling	pancakes
disco ball	sleepy	hopscotching	chili
tutu	soggy	winking	creamed corn

Mami Tucán called to Diego from high up in the _____

canopy of trees. "Diego, my babies are hungry, but I can't reach their nest

in the _____. All this _____ is causing too

much commotion!" Diego saw the trouble without needing the help of

Click the Camera or a _____: Two mischievous monkeys

were _____ over the baby toucans' nest. They didn't realize

they were causing so much trouble! "It's the Bobo Brothers," said Diego.

"Don't worry, Mami Tucán. Your babies won't have to eat _____

_____. We'll help." Then Diego shouted, "Freeze, Bobos!" The

Bobo Brothers stopped _____. "Whoops. Sorry," they said.

Now Mami Tucán could make sure her babies had a well-balanced meal

of _____ fruit and _____ insects.

MAD LIBS JUNIOR™ is fun to play with friends, but you can also play it by yourself! To begin, look at the story on the page below. When you come to a blank space in the story, look at the symbol that appears underneath. Then find the same symbol on this page and pick a word that appears below the symbol. Put that word in the blank space, and cross out the word, so you don't use it again. Continue doing this throughout the story until you've filled in all the spaces. Finally, read your story aloud and laugh!

"¡Hola! This is a very special story where you can help me rescue an animal in trouble! Whenever you see this symbol , write your name in the blank!"

MY ANIMAL RESCUE, PART 1

★ NOUNS	☺ ADJECTIVES	➡ VERBS	? MISC.
fork	purple	scuba dive	belly button
mustache	spotty	cha-cha	brain
paintbrush	crunchy	hopscotch	tummy
haystack	lumpy	jiggle	earlobe
megaphone	frumpy	hula	nose
magic wand	shiny	tango	eyeball
mirror	strange	skip	knee
underwear	gooey	spin	elbow
go-kart	wrinkly	twist	fingernail
handkerchief	plaid	flip	toe
pencil	goofy	bounce	thumb
beach ball	droopy	squawk	eyelash

Diego's electronic _____ says there's an animal in trouble!
★

It's a green iguana, and she's stuck in the most _____ part of
😎

the rain forest. Will you help Diego rescue her, _____?
✓

"¡Gracias, _____!" says Diego. First, Diego and _____
✓   ✓

need to _____ deep into the rain forest. "But how will we get
➡

over the giant _____ without a speedy _____?"
?   ★

Diego wonders. "We should jump," says _____. "Good idea,
✓

_____," says Diego. "¡Salta, salta! Jump, jump!" Oh, no.
✓

There's a _____ puma sleeping in the bushes. "We don't
😎

want to disturb the puma," says Diego. "Let's tiptoe quietly past him!"

Diego and _____ have made it through the rain forest in
✓

the blink of a/an _____. But where is the green iguana?
?

MAD LIBS JUNIOR™ is fun to play with friends, but you can also play it by yourself! To begin, look at the story on the page below. When you come to a blank space in the story, look at the symbol that appears underneath. Then find the same symbol on this page and pick a word that appears below the symbol. Put that word in the blank space, and cross out the word, so you don't use it again. Continue doing this throughout the story until you've filled in all the spaces. Finally, read your story aloud and laugh!

"¡Hola! This is a very special story where you can help me rescue an animal in trouble! Whenever you see this symbol ✓, write your name in the blank!"

MY ANIMAL RESCUE, PART 2

★ NOUNS	☺ ADJECTIVES	➡ VERBS	? MISC.
motorcycle	stormy	snorkeling	trained seals
pencil case	fuzzy	twirling	cowboys
pistachio	crazy	dancing	librarians
pet rock	bumpy	jitterbugging	ballerinas
race car	top-secret	honking	magicians
papaya	chocolate	bopping	acrobats
sweater vest	vanilla	singing	cockroaches
microscope	slimy	croaking	pirates
hula hoop	super-duper	hopping	dragons
mailbox	creaky	twirling	babysitters
marshmallow	ancient	spinning	fairies
model airplane	itchy	skipping	leprechauns

"*¡Ayúdame!*" cries the green iguana. There she is—_____ ➡ for

help in a deep hole. To get there, _____ ✓ and Diego need to

make it across the river. "What should we do?" asks Diego. "Let's swim!" says

_____ ✓. *¡Nada, nada!* Swim, swim! To get to the other side,

_____ ✓ and Diego swim like a pair of _____ ?. When

they reach the iguana, _____ ✓ ties a rope to the _____ ★

and throws it into the hole to help her out. "*¡Sube!*" _____ ✓ tells the

iguana, and she climbs out. "*Gracias*, _____ ✓ and Diego," says the

iguana. Suddenly, Diego's _____ ★ starts _____ ➡ with

a rescue call. "It's a flock of _____ ?," Diego says, "and they need

our help!" Go, Diego and go, _____ ✓, go! Now _____ ✓

is a/an _____ ✓ animal rescuer—just like Diego!